Couch

How to Write 50,000 Words in a Month,

Without Burning Out

Rachel Tonks Hill

Copyright © 2018 by Rachel Tonks Hill

All rights reserved. This book or any portion thereof may not be reproduced or used in any manner whatsoever without the express written permission of the publisher except for the use of brief quotations in a book review.

www.racheltonkshill.com

CONTENTS

Introduction 1
It's a marathon, not a sprint 8
Slow and Steady Wins the Race 14
It helps to Have Some Friends Along for the Ride 20
Find Your Zone and Get In It 26
Track Your Output For Best Results 34
What Counts As Writing? 41
The Couch to 50k Program 44
Some Tools to Help You On Your Way 64
Summary 75
About The Author 84
Other Books By The Author 85

INTRODUCTION

There are many people who, when pressed, will admit to a deep-seated desire to write a novel.

And yet, a vanishingly small number of those people ever actually make that dream a reality. Many people never even start. A few more people will admit to a half written draft languishing unloved in a drawer somewhere, or in a well-hidden folder on their computer.

Why do so many people who want to write a novel never do so?

Simply put, because Writing A Novel is hard.

Or rather, people *think* writing a novel is hard. In their heads it is this gargantuan, insurmountable task that they haven't a hope of completing, so why even try?

But if writing a novel is so hard, how is it that so many writers make a living doing just that? And these writers don't just write one novel, they write many. Some writers manage *hundreds* of novels over the course of their career.

So, obviously, writing a novel isn't completely

unattainable after all.

But for those who've never written a novel before, it can still seem like a daunting prospect because that's a lot of words.

Writing a novel is like any complex task: it can be broken down into many smaller tasks that are repeated until the larger task is complete. The smaller task in this case being something like "sit at your computer until words happen."

A novel is just words. You can write words.

And if you keep writing words, eventually you'll have written enough to call a novel.

This book aims to give you the tools you need to break down the task of Writing A Novel into something manageable. It's going to give you exactly what you need to get up off the couch and into your writing chair.

And, most importantly, it's going to give you what you need to *stay* there until you've written 50,000 words.

Why 50k?

The main answer to that is "because of NaNoWriMo."

NaNoWriMo, for those who aren't familiar, stands for National Novel Writing Month. Every November, thousands of writers from around the world commit to writing 50,000 words of a novel in a single month. From

00:01 on November 1st to 23:59 on November 30th, these writers dedicate their time and energy to doing what so many people dream of: writing a novel.

This book, therefore, gives you the tools necessary to complete NaNoWriMo, if that is your goal.

But even if doing NaNoWriMo isn't something you're interested in doing, writing 50,000 words is still a worthwhile goal.

50,000 words counts as a short novel according to most definitions, which is part of the reason it's the goal for NaNoWriMo. You don't have to write hundreds of thousands of words on order to write a novel, 50,000 is enough. Doesn't that feel more attainable already?

(For most definitions of novel that I'm aware of, 40,000 words is enough. But there's something satisfying about 50,000 as a number. Maybe it's because it seems closer to 100k, which is A Lot of Words, maybe it's because it's divisible by five. I don't know, I'm not a number wizard. It just somehow feels like more of an achievement, so 50,000 is the number we're aiming for.)

So, by following the advice in this book, you will be able to write a novel in a single month. Isn't that cool? Tick it off the bucket list!

That thing that so many people want to do but never start or finish? that can be done in the space of a month. And what's more, it can be done in under a month *by you*.

Who is this person making bold claims?

So, at this point you might be asking who am I to be giving you this advice?

Don't worry, I'm not offended. It's a fair question.

Well, I'm a writer who's done NaNoWriMo several times, both successfully and unsuccessfully and I've done the slightly less famous Camp NaNoWriMos as well, again with varying results.

I'm a writer who has obsessively tracked my daily word counts over the last few years and has, without committing to or even really trying, hit NaNoWriMo level word counts on a number of occasions. I've written novels and published them.

In fact, one of those novels is around 50,000 words long and was written in a month. So I know this is possible.

But above all else I'm a writer who believes that everyone who wants to write a novel can do so. All it takes is practice and a little determination.

The contents of this book are based on my experiences with NaNoWriMo, and with writing similar monthly word counts outside of November. If you can learn from the mistakes I've made, then hopefully you'll need to make fewer mistakes yourself on your journey to writing your novel.

And honestly, that's all I want.

What this book will give you

This book starts with some general advice on writing, focusing on the information you'll need to attempt 50,000 words in a month. These are things I've learned, often the hard way, about best practices on getting words down.

Don't skip this section. You'll need to keep in mind everything in this book if you want to write 50,000 words in a single month without crashing so hard you never want to think about writing ever again. That is not the fate I want for you.

In the first section we're going to focus on pacing, and why it's important. Seriously, it is So Important.

We're also going to cover why it can really help to have a friend along for the ride when attempting something like this. I'm also going to talk about getting into the "writing zone," and why being able to do so at will is essential to meeting any kind of writing goal.

I'll also cover a little bit about tracking the amount you write, and why it can be the difference between success and failure. There's also a section on what does and doesn't count as writing, to forestall any procrastination.

Then, in the second section, I'm going to give you what few other writing advice books do: an actual program that will help you meet our goals. You'll be able to choose whether to aim for writing 50,000 words in a month, as with NaNoWriMo, or whether you just want to write 50,000 words in total.

You'll be able to choose from three different programs, depending on the amount of time and effort you're willing to put in and how quickly you want to meet your goals. Each program will give you attainable goals for each week and will help you measure your progress as you work towards writing 50,000 words.

Whichever route you choose, you'll be given the tools and guidance necessary to work up to a successful NaNoWriMo, writing 50,000 words in a single month.

What this book is not

This book is not a writing craft book.

It will not give you any advice on plot, character, setting, scene composition, grammar, sentence construction or genre tropes. All of these are good things to know and learn about, but I'm not going to cover any of them in this book.

In fact, even though I've used the word "novel" several times in just this introduction, the program could just as easily be used to write a non-fiction book or a series of short stories.

That's because the only thing this book is concerned with is word count. It will train you to be able to get words down, consistently, and without burning out. What those words are doesn't actually matter. All that matters is that you're writing.

Because as long as you keep writing you will eventually finish that novel, or short story, or essay. If you follow the advice in this book you will be able to comfortably write 50,000 words in a single month and once you can do that, any writing dream you have is within your grasp.

And I guarantee, making those dreams come true is one of the best feelings in the world.

It's a Marathon, not a Sprint

So, you've committed to writing 50,000 words in a single month. What now?

Now you train, you prepare.

Think of this sort of writing challenge like running a long distance race. You wouldn't sign up to do the London Marathon and expect to run it without any preparation or training at all, at least not without causing yourself a serious injury.

Why should writing be any different?

Yeah okay, writing is a lot less physically demanding than running a marathon, but jumping into a large writing challenge with no prep is just as likely to do damage as running a marathon with no training.

Marathon runners start their training weeks or even months in advance, slowly building up their strength by increasing the distance they run and decreasing the time they do it in by increments. It takes careful planning, with plenty of time for rest and recovery built into the plan in order to avoid exhaustion and injury.

Those runners who don't take the time to prepare end up with injuries or they don't finish. Sometimes both.

NaNoWriMo needs marathon training and preparation

NaNoWriMo is pretty much the marathon of writing challenges, and it requires a similar mindset and approach to preparation as a marathon does. Just like with running a marathon, those writers who throw themselves into NaNoWriMo without thinking find themselves burning out in short order.

Many of them don't finish. Others end up burning out so badly they're put off writing for months or years.

I have one friend who succeeded in their first NaNoWriMo but was so exhausted by the end of it that they'll never attempt it again. And they haven't so much as looked at novel they started since then, even though it's pretty good.

This is the fate I want you to avoid.

If you think about it, it's rather obvious that jumping into NaNoWriMo like a kid at the deep end of the pool is going to end in burn out and disappointment (yes I'm mixing my metaphors there—deal with it). If you've not written anything but work emails in years it's going to be a struggle to write 50,000 words of *anything*, let alone in a single month. And the attempt is just as likely to end up with you hating writing as it is you successfully finishing 50,000 words.

Ramp it up slowly

Thinking about NaNoWriMo as a marathon instead of a sprint, it becomes obvious that you need to start preparing for it weeks if not months ahead of time.

And I'm not just talking about character development or story planning or world-building, although these are all good things to think about in the run up to November if you're writing a novel in the traditional sense of the word.

No, what I'm talking about is preparing for the hard work of actually doing the writing.

You need to start building the habit of writing every day so that it's not such a shock to the system come November 1st. You need to start carving out the time to write, and steadily increasing both the amount of time you spend writing and the amount you write in that time.

Finding time to write

Actually finding the time to write can be one of the hardest parts of a challenge like NaNoWriMo.

There are a billion and one distractions and energy-drains that life can throw at you that it's often hardest to get started. Most writers (ye, even professional ones) have a day job of some sort, which takes up a huge amount of time and energy.

But even when you get home there's a ton of things that seem to conspire to stop you sitting down to write. There's always dishes to be washed, laundry to be done, things to be dusted, kids to play with, spouses to spend quality time with and you should probably wash your hair at least once this week, right?

Finding the time to sit down and write, and guarding that time like it's priceless jewellery, is one of the hardest things about writing in my experience. That's why you need to start practising well ahead of November.

I promise you that if you can barely carve out ten minutes a week to write prior to NaNoWriMo, you're not going to be able to find the time to write more than 1500 words *every single day* in November.

Training. Practice.

It's just not going to happen otherwise.

Pacing is key

You need to think very carefully about pacing yourself when attempting to write 50,000 words in a single month.

Marathon runners don't run at the same lightening speed as Usain Bolt does. It's just not sustainable for that kind of long distance running.

Likewise, you're not going to be able to complete

NaNoWriMo by approaching it like a 2000 word college essay: dashed off in a single, sleepless night whilst eating your body weight in coleslaw directly from the tub. Ahem.

In order to avoid injury, and repetitive strain injury is a real risk when writing this sort of volume of words, you're going to have to pace yourself. Especially if you have a day job that requires lots of typing.

The same goes for avoiding burnout. If you pace yourself properly, by doing a little bit of writing every day, you've got a much better chance of succeeding than if you approach writing 50,000 words as a sprint.

You need a training program that'll get you there

In order to give yourself the best chance at succeeding at something like NaNoWriMo, you have to approach it like a marathon. I simply cannot overstate that.

You can't expect to go into it without any kind of practice or training and still somehow succeed. That's an excellent way to crash and burn so hard you never want to write for pleasure ever again, and pick up a wicked case of RSI into the bargain.

No, in order to write 50,000 words on a single month you need to start thinking about it weeks if not months ahead. You need to practice carving out time to write, and get good at defending it. You need to work at increasing the number of words you can get out within that time, and slowly increase the amount of time you spend writing until you're producing tne output necessary to win NaNoWriMo.

You need to spend some time working out where and how and when you write best, and that can only be done over a long period of time. You need to develop the habit of writing *every single day* so that you're not asking too much of yourself come November. You need to strengthen your writing muscles, and there's only one way to do that, and it's exactly the same way a runner strengthens the muscles they need for running.

Practice. Training. Preparation.

What you need is a program that will help you do all these things so that when it's time to sit down and write 50,000 words within a single month, you know you're capable of it.

A runner wouldn't dream of attempting a marathon without having gone through some kind of training program. Why are you attempting something like NaNoWriMo without a training program?

That's why I wrote this book, to give you the program you need. Let's get started shall we?

Slow and Steady Wins the Race

We've all heard of the story of the tortoise and the hare right?

The hare races against the tortoise and, because he's so much faster, he thinks he's going to have no problem winning. The hare, in his arrogance, takes a nap and ends up losing the race to the tortoise, who kept going the whole time.

It's probably the most famous of Aesop's fables and is often used to caution against over-confidence and praise doggedness and determination.

A New Twist in the Tale of the Tortoise and the Hare

I want you to imagine for a moment, a slightly different version of this race, with a much longer track. The hare, being made for running fast over short distances, takes off at full speed, leaving the tortoise behind.

But the hare quickly finds he can't sustain that speed for the entire distance, even though he pushes himself hard. Exhaustion sets in. The hare starts trembling with the effort of keeping going. Unable to push his mind or body any further, the hare crashes out of the race. And, because he pushed so hard, a brief rest doesn't do much to help him recover, and so he finds it difficult to join the race again.

The tortoise on the other hand, knowing her limitations, knowing that she's much better taking that kind of distance slowly but steadily, does a little of the course at a time and takes frequent rest. She's nowhere near as fast as the hare, but because she doesn't push herself so hard she almost collapses, the rests help her recover and she finds it much easier to start up again after a break. In the end she's the only one who ends up finishing the race.

Applying this Principle to NaNoWriMo

This version of the tortoise and the hare plays out hundreds of times all over the world every November. The race is NaNoWriMo, and the finish line is 50,000 words.

There are people who manage a whole bunch of words at the beginning, buoyed up by excitement at the start of the challenge like new gym-goers in January. Maybe they manage more than the minimum requirements those first few days, dashing off thousands of words in quick succession. They're excited by their progress, and convinced it's gonna be no problem hitting the 50,000 word mark.

But then life happens. They have a job to do, food to make, a house to clean, a family to spend time with. All these other things that require time and energy. Things that need doing, things that are a joy to do, but that cut into the time they have available to write. Combine the lack of time with a case of burnout from doing so much at the start and they fall off the writing wagon.

There's a chance that guilt might catch up with them or they might find another burst of energy to get one last flurry of words down at the end of the month, but it won't be enough to cross that 50,000 word finish line. And they'll be disheartened by their 'failure'.

In far too many cases this story leads to people never attempting NaNoWriMo again. Some people might even give up on writing altogether, having decided that they 'obviously' aren't cut out for it, and I think that's a real shame.

They won't see the words they *did* manage to get down as a success. They won't see that with a bit of planning and a determination to learn from their mistakes they could succeed next year.

Tortoises get Sh*t Done

At the same time there are hundreds if not thousands of people who take the tortoise approach to NaNoWriMo.

The tortoises work out how many words they need per day to succeed and resolve to write a little bit every day, aiming for what they need to stay on track. If they're in the mood they might write a little bit over that but won't push themselves too hard. Other days they might write a little bit less than the target but they know that's okay. Over the thirty days they focus on averaging enough words to complete the challenge. They don't despair.

The tortoise takes the slow and steady approach and works diligently to get words down without burning out. By practising careful pacing and looking after themselves when they're not writing, they get to the end of the month and hit that 50,000 word goal. Maybe they even have a few words more than that.

Buoyed up by their success, the tortoise is much more likely to try NaNoWriMo again in the future. And they're much more likely to keep writing in the meantime. The tortoise might even consider writing as a career or otherwise publishing what they've written to supplement their income. They're a lot less likely to quit writing forever.

Learn to be a Tortoise

What I want you to realise is that it's better to aspire to be a tortoise than a hare when it comes to writing. Consistently getting a few words down every day is always the better approach than sporadic spurts of a few thousand, and it's gonna lead to higher word counts overall.

It might feel good to write 3000 words in one go but if that's not sustainable for you then you're going to end up writing 3000 words just a few couple of times a month. On the other hand if you focus on a much more manageable goal of 1000 words a day, and hit that 20 days of the month, you'll have written way more than the sporadic writer.

The trouble tends to come when we see other people writing 3000 words in one go, and assume that they're doing that all the time.

There's a very human tendency to compare yourself with other people, especially during something like NaNoWriMo when people are being very open about their achievements. I need you to learn how to filter that out and focus on your own progress.

Sure, there are people who 'win' NaNoWriMo in the first day, but this requires spending a huge amount of time at the computer to the detriment of everything else, including sleep. It is most certainly not the norm and comes with an extremely high risk of burnout for those attempting it.

The truth is most people don't and can't do that. Hell, many people don't 'win' NaNoWriMo the first time around, and that's okay.

What I want more people to realise is that it's always a win to have more words at the end of the month that at the start, even if you didn't hit the number you were aiming for.

But if you're serious about writing 50,000 words in a single month you need to learn how to become a tortoise. You need to practice writing a little bit every day so that you'll hit your goal without relying on having to write a huge amount in a very short amount of time.

And you need a plan that is gonna help you do that.

Couch to 50k is that plan.

It helps to Have Some Friends Along for the Ride

One of the big draws of NaNoWriMo is the amount of support available from professional writers, other people doing the challenge and your friends. It doesn't really matter who it is, it's just important to have someone in your corner rooting for you.

But why is this so important?

Self-help and productivity gurus will tell you it's important to have a buddy with you because it provides an extra layer of accountability. And they're not wrong.

Accountability is Key

It's very easy to lie to yourself about what you have and haven't achieved and to give yourself way more slack than is reasonable. I'll be the first to admit I'm bad for this. I've ticked off tasks as done when they really aren't, or allowed myself the promised reward for work that's only mostly done, or is finished but sloppy.

It happens. It's human nature to want the reward, even if it's just the sense of accomplishment of ticking something off your to do list.

The point is it's super difficult when you're only accountable to yourself. It takes discipline and honesty and the ability to realistically evaluate what you've done.

Which are all things that your friends are better at doing for you.

When you've committed to something as psychologically intimidating as writing 50,000 words in a single month it's even harder to remain honest. I mean, if you can say you've taken the trash out *when it's still sat right there in your kitchen* (innocent whistling abounds) then how easy is it going to be to fool yourself into believing you've done more writing than you have?

Or that you've done writing when all you've actually done is spent the last hour playing solitaire?

Having a friend (or two) rooting for you provides you with a barrier to self-deception. As a general rule we feel way worse about lying to people we love than we do lying to ourselves. Which means you're a lot less likely to do it.

Friends are Good for Motivation Too

So, having a friend who knows what you've promised yourself, who'll check in with you every day can be a huge motivator. They don't even have to be doing NaNoWriMo themselves, though if you can drag them along with you that'll help even more. There's something to be said for facing adversity together and if the worst comes to the worst you can commiserate with your friend about your suffering and poor life choices etc.

But even if you can't scrounge up a mate willing to do NaNoWriMo alongside you, it still helps to have someone there for you. Someone to keep you accountable, and honest with yourself. Who'll encourage you to hit your daily goals and commiserate when you don't quite get there.

Someone who knows that doing *some* writing is better than not doing any, even if you don't quite do as much as you wanted to.

Having someone along for the ride also provides a sense of community. In fact, in my experience, that sense of community is one of NaNoWriMo's greatest strengths.

One is the Loneliest Number

Writing is an inherently lonely process. Most of the time it's just you sat at the computer or with your pen and paper as you make shit up. I find I concentrate better with headphones on and music playing, which just enhances the sense of isolation, even if I'm writing in a room with other people present.

Even when in company, writing is mostly down to you, and you alone. Alone with your thoughts as you grapple with characters and plot and setting and try to weave magic with your words.

That loneliness can get to you after a while.

So knowing someone else is there really helps. It makes the whole process more fun and provides an incentive to keep going when things are tough. You can share your successes and failures, the highs and lows of writing together.

And if nothing else works, you can guilt each other into getting shit done. Guilt can be a great motivator believe me.

Getting yourself a writing buddy can make a huge differences to your chances of success with something like NaNoWriMo.

Online Friends Count Too

Having someone you know in meatspace (instead of, you know on the interwebs) is just one option though. For some people it might be the best option, but it's not the only one. If you can't persuade any of your meatspace friends to do NaNoWriMo with you, or even just to check in with you every day (at which point you might need to consider new friends, just sayin') then there are other places to find a writing buddy.

You could join a writing group, either on or offline. Check your local ads to see if there are any local meet ups for writers that you can get to. Even if there isn't a regular group, there might be some NaNoWriMo specific meetings you could attend.

And even if you're somehow the only writer for 50 miles, there are tons of online writing groups you could try. I've lost count of the number of Facebook writing groups I've seen, and you can always go searching for Ye Olde Chatrooms or forums.

If you're more of a twitter person than anything else there are a bunch of ways to find people to write with. The official NaNoWriMo hashtags are always worth a look, and there are probably local variations to help you find other writers who are in the same time zone as you at least. And there are people on twitter who run regular writing sprints during November to help you met your goals. Check out things like #amwriting to find people to connect with outside of NaNoWriMo.

And if all else fails you could always ask your mum to ask for your word count every week. I know you won't lie to her.

Competition Isn't always Good

A word of caution though, especially if your writing buddy is doing the challenge alongside you: be wary of comparisons. It's all too easy to compare ourselves and our accomplishments and our outputs with other people, and to want to come out on top. Some level of competition can be really useful, as long as it's encouraging and not getting you down.

Don't use comparison with your writing buddy as something to beat yourself up about is what I'm saying.

This can be difficult, especially if your buddy is writing more than you. I've been on both sides of this and yeah, it's hard if you're the one who has fewer words. It feels like you're falling behind, and your brain starts using words like 'failure' at you.

Just be wary of falling into that trap and practice being kind to yourself. Remember that a little bit of competition and friendly rivalry is fine, as long as you're encouraging each other to do better and hit your goals, but ultimately something like NaNoWriMo is a competition against *yourself*.

You're doing this because you want to write more than you did before and that's great. Have someone to keep you accountable to the goal you've set yourself but be realistic about it.

And if you find yourself mentally beating yourself up because you've not written as much as your buddy has, just remember: the most important thing is that you get words down. If you have more words at the end of the month than you did at the beginning than you've already won.

No matter what else might happen.

FIND YOUR ZONE AND GET IN IT

In order to give yourself the best chance of succeeding at NaNoWriMo, you need to find your zone.

Your "zone" is that mental space where you do your best work. Where the words come to you easily and you trust in your ability to do what you're doing and do it well.

In other words, your zone is the place where your words *flow*.

What Is Flow?

Flow is actually a psychology term coined in 1975 by Mihály Csíkszentmihályi to describe a particular state of mind. Flow happens when a person performing a task is fully immersed in that task and experiences a sense of energised focus and enjoyment of the process of carrying out said task.

I've seen the flow state described as that point where the difficulty of a task perfectly matches your ability level, such that you can become absorbed in that task without requiring conscious thought. Any time you've found yourself lost in an activity, unaware of time passing or what's happening around you, you've been in a state of flow.

Flow is exactly what's happening when the writing's good, when the words seem to pour from your fingertips like magic and you're flying on the wings of your own creation. If you want to make writing a daily habit, the sort that will let you rack up word counts like those demanded by NaNoWriMo, you need to make sure as many of your writing sessions feel like flying as possible.

Enjoying the Act of Writing

Because that part about *enjoying the process* of completing the task that you're flowing with? That's the super important bit for writing. Because it's the enjoyment of the writing process that's going to keep you coming back to your desk day after day.

George R.R. Martin (you know, the guy who writes Game of Thrones) has famously said that he doesn't enjoy writing, he enjoys having written. At which point I wonder why the hell he went into writing as a career in the first place.

And I'll be honest, if he really doesn't enjoy writing as a process, it's no wonder it's taking him so long to write his next book.

A quick google search will turn up several more examples of writers claiming similar things. That they don't enjoy the process of writing, they enjoy having done it.

Let me be absolutely, brutally honest: if you don't enjoy the process of writing, you might want to have a think about exactly why you want to write. Because if you don't enjoy the actual writing part of writing, you're not going to much enjoy writing a novel or attempting NaNoWriMo.

So, before you go any further, have a think about *why* you want to write. Do you want to be a writer, a person who's job it is to write every day? Or do you want to write so you can be the next J.K. Rowling or Andy Weir or whoever ends up making it big with their debut novel in six months' time? Because the odds are super not in your favour if that's the case.

If you're the sort of person who only enjoys writing in the past tense, you're going to struggle with something like NaNoWriMo. Because in order to hit that all important word count you're going to have to sit down and actually write every single day of the month.

And if the thought of that fills you with dread then you really do need to do some thinking about whether this sort of challenge is right for you.

Optimize your Environment

At a minimum you're gonna have to spend some time working out the optimum conditions that are gonna let you sit down in that chair every day and fucking write. Because that is the only thing that is gonna get those 50,000 words written within a month. I promise you that it will be time well spent, because armed with the knowledge of where, when and how you do your best writing, and achieve maximum enjoyment while doing it, you'll be unstoppable.

Professional writers and successful NaNoWriMoers alike (and the significant crossover between the two groups) have all taken the time necessary to really optimise their writing conditions. And if you're serious about writing 50,000 words in a month then you're gonna have to do the same.

Because, irritatingly, those optimum conditions are different for every writer.

Asking the Important Questions

I wish I could tell you exactly how to find your zone, I really do. If I could give you a fifteen point checklist that would guarantee you'd be able to knock out 2000 words every single day if you followed it, then believe me I would. Sadly it's not as simple as that.

So, in order to find out how *you* write best, you're going to have to ask yourself some questions.

Do you work better writing on a computer or long hand with pen and paper? Or can you get more done if you use speech-to-text software and dictate your words?

Does having music playing help or hinder your

creative process? And if you work better with music do you know which genre is best suited? Does the style of music change depending on what you're writing? And of course there's the question of whether to use speakers or headphones.

What does your ideal workspace look like? Are you going to find it easier to sit down and write if you have a dedicated workspace, or are you the sort of person who prefers writing in coffee shops or other public places? If you have a writing desk does it need to be tidy and well organised or does your creativity thrive in a little chaos?

If you're going with the traditional typing route then some thought as to program might be useful. Do you just want to stick with something tried and true like Word or do you want something that's more specialised for writing like Scrivener? Will something minimalistic suit you better so you don't have to deal with distractions? Is it worth trying a writing program that has penalties for stopping or slowing down your typing such as Write or Die?

Can you concentrate on your writing when you have access to the internet or are you going to have to turn it off at the router so you can concentrate?

And then there's the time of day to consider, not just in terms of when you write best, but also when you have *time* to write. If you're a natural morning person (and how I envy you) then you might be better off trying to get up earlier if you're struggling to get some writing in.

But if you're more of a night owl then not only is this likely to be counterproductive, you're less likely to do your best work if you'd rather be in bed. Do your writing in the evening, or try to get a few words done.

And remember, if you're really crunched for the time and energy to make words happen, the time you'll do your best writing is whenever you can fit some in. Write a few words on your phone every time you have five minutes to spare if you have to.

Getting into the Zone on Command

Once you know the answers to these questions you need to work on creating your optimum conditions and practising getting into your zone on command. Train your brain to understand that when you sit down in these conditions, you are here to write, and it needs get those creative juices running.

Set up some sort of ritual for the start of your writing sessions, a set of actions that you do every time you go to write, something that will trigger your ability to focus on the task at hand. Maybe you'll decide to light a particular scented candle or play your favourite song or brush your teeth. It doesn't matter what that trigger is, as long as you have something that tells your brain it's time to put some words down.

For me, I tend to find I can get a lot of writing done if I have a couple hours in a morning. I sit at my computer, boot up one of my minimalist writing apps (my favourites keep changing, but FocusWriter and WriteMonkey have been on the roster for a while now) and stick my headphones on. I have a playlist of three albums by one of my favourite bands that I know so well I can largely tune the lyrics out and focus on what I'm writing. I know when my headphones are on and the music starts, it's time to get down to business.

Remember things Change

Set some time aside to work out what your optimum conditions for writing are. It's also worth working out the conditions that let you do pretty well, because your optimum writing time might not always be available to you. That's why the ritual can be powerful, because it can tell your brain it's time to write even if you're not in the usual place and circumstances.

People are changeable as well, so keep that in mind when carving out your time. You might not always get the same results from the same setting, and your optimum conditions can change over time, especially as you train your brain to write on command. Try to stay flexible and have a number of less optimum but still good options you can fall back on.

And remember, the best time to write is the time you have, so if all you've got is ten minutes on the bus at 5am, take it. We don't always have the luxury of the perfect environment and you may have to work out how to get writing out in some weird places.

It is absolutely worth it to build the habit of writing

every day. A little bit every day can add up to a whole lot, as you'll see in the next chapter.

Track Your Output For Best Results

Once you've found your zone, you need to work out how productive you can be when you're in it. And as far as the challenge of writing 50,000 words in a month is concerned, productivity is how many words you can get down in a given time slot.

WPH (Words Per Hour)

Take half an hour out of your day to sit down (or stand, if you're one of those fancy people with a standing desk) and do a couple of sprints. Write as much as you can for ten minutes, or fifteen or twenty-five, whatever feels right to you. Just write as much as you can for that time without distractions and then count up how much you got done.

I find I need to do a quick proof and spellcheck before I count, because I write in a program that doesn't highlight my spelling and typing errors. Going back to fix minor mistakes like that is absolutely a distraction and will pull you out of your flow. Don't do it.

Count up how much you got done and then do it again. Do a few sprints to work out what suits you, whether you perform better in shorter spurts or longer sessions, but try not to type for more than an hour at a time. Your wrists will thank you for taking breaks.

Once you've got your word count for that session (or group of sessions) you absolutely need to record it.

Why?

I'll tell you.

Logging Your Performance

Going back to the marathon analogy, runners who are serious about their training keep logs of their performance. The distance they ran on a particular day and how long it took them to do it. If you do both those things you can work out your average pace, which is useful for estimating how long it might take you to cover longer distances. Some runners with fancy devices even keep track of their pace for different parts of their route, which can highlight things they're still struggling with and suggest areas for improvement.

If you're training for the marathon of the writing world, you absolutely need to track your output, because you're going to have to do that during NaNoWriMo anyway.

Sure you can just sit down and type and hope for the best, only counting up your total at the end of the month, but that's a road paved with disappointment and failure.

Humans will almost always overestimate their achievements, and following this route is likely to end with you *thinking* you've hit 50k when you actually haven't. And it is absolutely no good just thinking you've hit 1700 words per day or 50,000 words in a month if you haven't. You need to *know*.

Being mistaken about your exact word count is almost certainly gonna end with you never wanting to try NaNoWriMo ever again, and in extreme cases, quitting writing altogether.

By this point you've put way too much effort in to let yourself miss your goals because you weren't properly tracking your output.

Track Your Total Daily Word Count At Least

At a bare minimum you need to track your total word count for every day you write. Bare minimum.

I would advise keeping more detailed records if you can, because just like for our marathon running friend, having information on your pace can be invaluable. Keeping records of the amount of time spent writing, the number of words written, number of sessions the time of day you were writing, your location and even your mood can be useful information.

Some of those items will help you nail down your ideal conditions for writing as discussed in the previous chapter, and can tell you a lot about you as a writer, but I've not found it necessary in my own writing practice. As ever though, your mileage may vary.

Keeping a record of your total word count and the time you spent writing can give you an edge come November though, because it can help you work out your average number of words per hour. That's your writing pace and can be crucial information when it comes to attempting NaNoWriMo.

If you know you can write 1000 words in an hour, factoring in breaks, then you know you'll need to set aside two hours everyday in order to make the NaNoWriMo daily word goal. And knowing how much time you need makes it easier to actually get that time in the writing chair. Schedule it, get up early, tell your family you need quiet time, do whatever you need to do to get your ass in your writing chair for that two hours you need.

You Don't Need To Do It All At Once

Do bear in mind though that you don't need to do your two hours (or however long you've worked out need) in one go. If you can grab half an hour first thing in the morning, half an hour at lunch and an hour in the evening, that's fine.

As long as you're carving out enough time and

you're actually writing for that time, then you'll hit your daily goals.

And the more you write, the quicker you're likely to make your word count. Not necessarily because your typing speed has improved (though I absolutely recommend trying to improve how fast you can type if you're serious about your writing) but because it gets easier to get into your zone the more you practice.

You'll spend less time staring into space wondering why the words won't come and more time just writing. It's all about practice.

That brings me to another reason why keeping records is super useful: it can really help with habit building. And that's ultimately what this book is about, helping you build a writing habit that'll get you to your goal.

Building Positive Habits

The best way to build a new habit is to do it every day. Realistically, you're gonna miss days here and there, and that's okay. Be gentle with yourself if you absolutely cannot do any writing on a particular day. Just pick yourself back up the next day and try again. For best results in building a new habit, try not to miss more than one day in a row.

If you're keeping records of how much you're writing the evidence of how well you're doing is right there. You can tell how many days in a row you've managed to write and whether you managed to get back on the writing horse quickly after a missed day. You know how well you're doing because you've got the data right there.

Just as important to building a new habit as daily practice is celebrating your success. It's that little hit of dopamine when you get your words done that's gonna keep you coming back again and again.

So celebrate when you have a really good writing day, when you knock it out of the park word count wise. Celebrate when you manage to get some words down despite feeling cruddy. Celebrate when you get a really nice streak going.

It doesn't have to be anything big. Give yourself a sticker, pat yourself on the back. Just do something that celebrates your successes and you'll keep building on them.

That Warm Sense Of Accomplishment

Keeping records of how much you're writing can really give you a sense of accomplishment. Sure, 500 words might not feel like a lot when you're actually doing them (or it might, and that's okay too) but if you manage that every day it sure adds up.

Writing 500 words every single day will net you around 15000 words a month. Keeping that up for a whole year will result in 180,000 words. Does that feel like a lot now?

A little bit every day really adds up in the long run, ant by keeping track of your word counts you can see that with your own eyes. You might be surprised by how much you're actually getting done.

Seeing your achievements in concrete data is gonna give you that little hit of endorphins that'll make building a writing habit that much easier. And it's that habit that is gonna enable you to write 50,000 words in a single month.

What Counts As Writing?

Before we actually get into the Couch to 50k program itself, I want to have a quick talk about what actually counts as writing for the purposes of your records. And I'm gonna be really mean here, but in the long run it's going to help you be more honest with yourself and fend off procrastination.

So, what actually counts writing that you can include in your word count?

Writing is adding brand new words to any project you're working on that results in a measurable increase in your word count.

That's it. Sounds simple right?

Just put more words on the page so that whatever program you're writing in tells you you have more words at the end of the session than you did at the beginning.

Now, just so we're absolutely clear on where we stand, here are a bunch of things that do **not** count as writing.

- Planning out new scenes, chapters, stories etc.

- Editing, except for when you're adding new words to a project on a second pass.
- Research for whatever it is that you're writing. If it involves spending long stretches of time on Wikipedia, it's not writing.
- Proofreading to eliminate spelling, typing or formatting errors.
- Spending time on Twitter, Facebook or any other social media, even if you're talking to other writers.
- Checking your email for the fifteenth time that day.
- Reading writing craft books.
- Copying and pasting from your plans, previous iterations of your current project, abandoned works, other peoples work etc.
- Daydreaming, even if you're thinking about the writing project you're currently working on.
- Taking the dog for a walk because she's been giving you *that look* for hours.
- Washing the dishes because they've been in the sink for three days and you're worried they've become sentient.
- Finally painting the kitchen after ten years not being able to pick a colour.
- Deleting an entire scene, chapter, section of your project because you've decided you hate it.
- Literally anything that isn't adding new words to your project.

Now don't get me wrong, some of those not-writing activities are essential pre or post writing or for maintaining good self care. I'm not making the case that you shouldn't edit or proofread your work, or that you need to leave the dishes to evolve. Definitely take the dog for a walk at some point.

What I am saying is that for the purposes of habit building and recording your output, the only thing I am concerned with is the time you spend adding new words to a project in such a way that the project's overall word count increases.

That's it.

That is the only thing that counts as writing time. Anything else is procrastination.

The Couch to 50k Program

So here we are, this is where we put everything together in a program designed to get you from writing nothing to being able to take on the challenge of NaNoWriMo.

The Couch to 50k program gives you a concrete number of words to shoot for every day, focusing on improving your writing stamina and building the habit of writing every day. Even if you're not shooting for a NaNoWriMo style challenge, this program will help you meet whatever writing goal you have. It'll help you start again after a period of no writing, and it'll help a beginner develop their confidence and skill.

Couch to 50k comprises of three programs designed to let you go at your own pace. The standard program happens over four weeks and will build you up from writing just 100 words on the first day to 1700 words a day in the final week. It's the ideal warm up for NaNoWriMo and will allow you to hit the ground running come November 1st and greatly improve your chances of getting to 50k.

The standard program is four weeks because it

takes around a month for a new habit to really settle in. That said, the standard program might not be for everybody so I've also developed two alternative programs; a gentler six week program for those who want to take a little longer to get up to speed and really work on building their writing habit, and a fast track 21 day program for those who want to get results quicker.

All three programs ask you to write every day, and they do that for a reason.

This program isn't just about winning NaNoWriMo, it's about training yourself to think like a writer. That means putting work into building a writing habit that will last you long past November 30th and help you achieve whatever writing dreams you have. In my experience, the best way to do that is to practice writing every day.

Doing something every day is a highly effective way to build a habit. If you shoot for doing *some* writing daily it doesn't matter if you miss a day because life happened. Just try to pick yourself up and start again the next day, no worries. Just try not to miss more than one day in a row or you're at risk of making *not* writing your new habit. Missing one day of writing is no big deal, and I encourage you to forgive yourself if it happens.

Compare that to if you were just writing three days a week, say Monday, Wednesday, Friday. If you forget to do your writing on the Friday, you're going a long time without putting any words down. Sure you could try to make up for your missed day, but if you don't have a daily habit backing you up that's going to be harder. Going so many days without writing isn't going to be as useful for helping you build good habits.

Writing every day is also the best way to break down a challenge like NaNoWriMo. 50,000 words is a lot to get done, but it sounds a lot less scary when you know that equates to 1670 words every day. The person who writes three times a week is only going to have about 12 writing days during November, depending on what days they write and how the calendar falls. That means they're going to have to write more than 4000 words every time they sit down, which is a heck of a lot more daunting than just over 1500.

Practice writing every day during Couch to 50k and you're gonna have a much better shot at getting those 50,000 words down in a single month, believe me.

Couch to 50k Base Program

This is the standard program that will get you up to NaNoWriMo speeds in just four weeks. The target word count starts out small and builds each day until you're writing 1700 words a day—more than enough to hit 50,000 words in a month. The program is designed to give you a little leeway, meaning that if you miss a few days during NaNoWriMo you don't have to scrabble as hard to catch back up.

Week One

This week is all about building the habit of daily writing. It starts off nice and gentle so that it's almost more work to *avoid* doing your writing than it is to just get it done. By the end of this week you will be comfortably writing 500 words a day, almost a third of the way to your ultimate goal.

Day	Target Word Count
1	100
2	200
3	300
4	400
5	500
6	500
7	500

Total words written this week: **2500** Overall total: **2500**

Week Two

This week you'll be building on your good habits from week one while gradually increasing your daily word count. By the end of this week you'll be writing 1000 words per day. This will put you two thirds of the way to your eventual daily word count, and is enough words per day to write a novella in a single month.

Day	Target Word Count
1	500
2	600
3	700
4	800
5	900
6	1000
7	1000

Total words written this week: **5500** Overall total: **8000**

Week Three

This week is about getting up to 1500 words per day. You're so close to your goal now, and you're building a really solid writing habit along the way. 1500 words per day would result in more than half a million words over the course of a year, with plenty of leeway for life getting in the way. Pat yourself on the back, you're really doing it!

Day	Target Word Count
1	1100
2	1200
3	1300
4	1400
5	1500
6	1500
7	1500

Total words written this week: **9500** Overall total: **12000**

Week Four

This is the final week of Couch to 50k, and it's time to go for broke. You've got a real handle on your writing habit by this point and making the jump from 1500 to 1700 words per day shouldn't be too hard. This week you're going to write the same amount every day to really build the stamina you need for NaNoWriMo and to reinforce all that habit building you've been doing.

Repeat this week three more times and guess what? You'll have won NaNoWriMo!

Day	Target Word Count
1	1700
2	1700
3	1700
4	1700
5	1700
6	1700
7	1700

Total words written this week: **11900** Overall total: **24900** (halfway to NaNoWriMo!)

Couch to 50k Fast Track Program

This is a 21 day program to get you up to speed much more quickly. It's not as good for building long term writing habits, but it still makes a great warm up for NaNoWriMo. The fast track program is ideal for experienced writers who've had a break from writing and are looking to get back into it. Or maybe you're just strapped for time and want to see results fast. Whatever your reasons, this program will get you up to NaNoWriMo speed on just three weeks.

You'll start out writing 100 words on the first day, and build on that until you hit 1700 words per day on day 17. The rest of the time is spent practising doing 1700 words every day to start building the habit you'll need for NaNoWriMo.

Week One

Just because you're on the fast track program doesn't mean you're not starting off gently. This first week is about getting used to writing every day, starting with some nice small word counts. You'll add 100 words to your target every day and by the end of the week you'll be in 700 words in a day, almost half way to your ultimate goal. Don't rush it any more than you have to. You'll get there.

Day	Target Word Count
1	100
2	200
3	300
4	400
5	500
6	600
7	700

Total words written this week: **2800** Overall total: **2800**

Week 2

In week two you're going to work on ramping up from 700 words to 1400 words in a single day. That's double your word count! And potentially 1400 more words than you were getting done before Couch to 50k. Add 100 words every day like last week, and work on not skipping any days this week. Next week will feel even harder if you skip days now.

Day	Target Word Count
8	800
9	900
10	1000
11	1100
12	1200
13	1300
14	1400

Total words written this week: **7700** Overall total: **10500**

Week 3

This week you'll work up to 1700 words a day—not a huge increase from 1400. Then you'll spend the rest of the week working at that level, practising and getting comfortable with doing that amount of words in a day. Congratulations, you've made it to the end of the fast track Couch to 50k Program. Just keep doing what you're doing and you'll make it to the end op NaNoWriMo and your novel on no time.

Day	Target Word Count
15	1500
16	1600
17	1700
18	1700
19	1700
20	1700
21	1700

Total words written this week: 11600 Overall total: **22100**

Couch to 50k Gentle

This is a six week program that is ideal for beginner writers or those who need to build up their confidence with writing. It starts nice and gentle with just 50 words on the first day. You'll add to that slowly over the course of five weeks and then spend a week writing 1700 words every day to really ingrain the habit and develop enough stamina for NaNoWriMo.

Week One

Day one of the gentle program only asks you to write 50 words; a small enough goal that it's almost more effort to avoid doing it than it is to get the words done. That is intentional, I promise. You'll then add 50 words to you target everyday and by the end of the week you'll not only have 1400 words under your belt, you'll also be getting comfortable with writing a little bit every day.

Day	Target Word Count
1	50
2	100
3	150
4	200
5	250
6	300
7	350

Total words written this week: **1400** Overall total: **1400**

Week Two

In week two you're going to keep adding fifty words every day until you're doing 700 words on day 7. The focus is still on just sitting down to do your words every day, practising and forming the habit that will see you through the larger word counts. By the end of this week you'll have written almost 4000 words, more than double what you did the previous week! Keep writing everyday day and adding more words slowly; the word counts will soon add up.

Day	Target Word Count
1	400
2	450
3	500
4	550
5	600
6	650
7	700

Total words written this week: **3850** Overall total: **5250**

Week Three

This week is going to get you past the 1000 word mark for a day's writing. Don't let that number put you off. You have two weeks of daily writing under your belt and you've got here slowly, so it shouldn't feel like a huge task. If you do feel like you're struggling with 1000 words a day, repeat this week a couple of times until you're used to it. You're on the gentle program here, there's no rush to the finish line. Just focus on building your writing habit; the rest will come.

Day	Target Word Count
1	750
2	800
3	850
4	900
5	950
6	1000
7	1050

Total words written this week: **6300** Overall total: **11550**

Week Four

This week is going to take you from that 1000 words in a day milestone to writing 1400 words in a day. That's just 300 words short of your ultimate goal. By the end of this week you'll have written over 20,000 words overall on the program; that's enough for a short novella! See how the words add up when you focus on small goals which increase gently and combine that with a daily habit? Keep adding 50 words a day and you'll be at NaNoWriMo speed in no time.

Day	Target Word Count
1	1100
2	1150
3	1200
4	1250
5	1300
6	1350
7	1400

Total words written this week: **8750** Overall total: **20300**

Week Five

By the end of this week you'll be writing 1700 words in a day! The jump from 1400 words to 1700 words is a small one, but take it as gently as before. Your focus with this program is to really form a writing habit that will get you where you want to go. Don't worry too much about the daily word counts themselves, they're increasing by the same amount they always have. By now you should more than have the stamina for around 1500 words a day but if not, if you're still struggling, feel free to go back and repeat a week.

Day	Target Word Count
1	1450
2	1500
3	1550
4	1600
5	1650
6	1700
7	1700

Total words written this week: **11150** Overall total: **31450**

Week Six

This there's no increase in word count, you're just going to write 1700 words every day to get used to writing at that level consistently. After six weeks of writing every day, and nine days of doing 1700 words per day, NaNoWriMo should be no problem. And if you've done this six week program you've already written more than 40,000 words overall. That's enough for a short novel already. Keep writing, and whatever you want to achieve with your writing will happen. And if you ever get out of the habit of writing, you can always come back and redo this program, or parts of it. Or try one of the others. You know you can do it now.

Day	Target Word Count
1	1700
2	1700
3	1700
4	1700
5	1700
6	1700
7	1700

Total words written this week: **11900** Overall total: **43350**

Choose whichever program feels best for you right now. You can always change it up and do one program after the other. Or the regular program might suit you best now but you may need to use the gentler one in the future to get back into writing. These programs are designed to suit *your* needs right now.

What happens if you get stuck on a program or fall off the wagon part way through?

Well, the first thing you need to do is work on forgiving yourself for it. It's okay, it happens. Sometimes life comes at you faster than you can handle it and something's got to give. Just get back to your writing whenever you can.

After that you've got a few options. Try repeating the last week of this program you completed successfully and see if you can move on from there. Alternately you can spend a week writing the last word count you got to so that you're comfortable with that output and really getting into the habit of writing that much every day.

If it takes you more than a couple of weeks to get back to writing you may be better off restarting the program, or at least going back a couple of weeks and starting there.

Remember, when I put these programs together I wanted it to be about more than just preparing for NaNoWriMo although doing Couch to 50k is a great way to do that. This is also about you building a lasting writing habit that's going to get you where you want to go. By starting off small and building on that you're going to have the confidence you need to tackle larger projects and the habits you need to complete them.

And if you are doing Couch to 50k to get in shape

for November, consider this: if you can write 50,000 words in a single month, what can't you do? You don't have to write that much every month but if you've developed the discipline, stamina and habits necessary to reach that goal then there are very few writing projects that are beyond you.

Just something to bear in mind.

So, choose a program and stick to it for the allotted time. Pick yourself back up and try again if you miss a day (and believe me, you will). Don't sweat the small mistakes because it's never worth it in the long run. Focus on building those habits.

I've given you the numbers, told you what you have to do to hit your goals, now lets get you the tools you're gonna need to succeed.

Some Tools to Help You On Your Way

Now it's all well and good to say "just write this many words per day for a few weeks and you'll be able to do NaNoWriMo no problem" and send you on your merry way. That is, as long as I don't care about making sure you succeed, which I do.

In my experience knowing what you have to do and actually doing it are completely different things. Whatever your level of experience, writing 50,000 words in a month is a big ask, and you're gonna need some support. You need a few tools on your belt that'll give you the best possible chance if succeeding.

A hammer with which to "smash it" as it were.

(I'm sorry, I'll never say that ever again.)

The Couch to 50k Program is about more than just telling you how many words to write and for how long. It's about equipping you with what you need to get where you want to go.

That's where this chapter comes in.

If the previous chapter was the nitty, gritty, numbers bit of Couch to 50k, then this chapter is about the resources you're likely to need to actually do what I've asked of you.

Let's see what shinies Q has for you today then shall we?

Word Count Trackers and More

Spreadsheets glorious spreadsheets! I love a good spreadsheet me, and over the last few years they've become indispensable when it comes to hitting my writing goals.

Now bear with me a moment.

I dedicated a whole chapter to the importance of tracking your writing output and keeping records of other potentially useful writing related data. Well fear not! I'm not expecting you to go away and write a spreadsheet that does everything you could possibly ask of it and more. I've put together a few that you can use and modify if you wish. They're not all that complicated (mostly because I can't do anything complicated in a spreadsheet; to this day I have no idea how macros work or what a pivot table is) but they will get you started.

The Couch to 50k Tracker

This is probably the most important spreadsheet in the list, which is why it's going first.

The Couch to 50k Tracker can be used to keep a record of your progress, no matter which version of the program you choose. It distils everything I told you in the last chapter into one handy dandy spreadsheet, and includes space for a few other useful bits of information as well, such as how far through the program you are and where each writing session took place.

If you only use one of the tools in this chapter, make sure it's this one. Following the program and recording your progress with this tracker really will give you your best shot at writing 50,000 words in a single month.

The Find Your Zone Tracker

This is a great tool if you want to find out how, where and when you do your best writing. Keep track of how long you write for, how many words you managed as well as other variables like time of day, location and mood. There's plenty of room for you to add your own data too, so you can really hone in on your ideal environment for getting words down.

The NaNoWriMo Tracker

This is where you're gonna get your writing marathon done. Thirty days of writing to get to that magical 50,000 words.

The NaNoWriMo Tracker is what's going to get you from a successful Couch to 50k program to being a NaNoWriMo winner. Like Couch to 50k, it breaks

NaNoWriMo down into manageable chunks and makes it easy to see how many words you have left to get down, whether you're behind or ahead of schedule and when you can expect to cross the finish line.

This tracker is also designed so that you can drag your friends along with you. Upload it to Google Docs or something and give them access, and you'll be able to record your progress together and introduce a little friendly competition if you want.

See how you're doing in comparison to your friends at a glance but remember, the real competition is again yourself and that big old number you're shooting for.

The Yearly Tracker

I've said it over and over again that Couch to 50k is not just about getting you up to speed for NaNoWriMo and giving you the best chance of succeeding. It's also about helping you build a sustainable, long-term writing habit that's gonna help you hit whatever writing goals you have beyond writing those 50,000 precious words in November.

This is where I put my money where my mouth is.

This tracker is based on the spreadsheet I myself use to track my writing output and make sure I'm hitting my goals. It has enough room for recording 365 days of writing, no matter what you're working on. You can use this spreadsheet no matter when in the year you start, and it includes space for setting some goals and working out how much progress you've made towards them.

I really hope you find this tracker as useful as I have over the last few years and I'm really excited to share it with you.

You can get your Couch to 50k trackers here: bit.ly/C250kTrackers

Useful Books

Now, I make no claims to being the only expert on writing and this is by no means the only book you might find useful on your journey to writing 50,000 words in a month. There are probably thousands of books on writing out there, but here are a handful I've found useful to have in my own toolbox.

Please note that I'm not getting anything in return for recommending these books to you, they're just books I've found helpful in my own writing.

The Write Attitude and The Pursuit of Perfection by Kristine Kathryn Rusch

These two books kind of go hand in hand with each other, and if you only grab one of the books on this list, make sure it's one of these.

Both these books focus on the attitude and mindset of the writer, and I have found them both absolutely indispensable for my own writing. It's far too easy to get caught up in expectation as a writer, and feel like a failure when your experience doesn't line up with that of other writers. Whenever that happens to me I like to pull this book out as an antidote.

The truth is every writer is different, and comparing your life, output, income, methods or number of awards to anyone else's is a futile endeavour that's just going to make you sad. These books will help with the attitude adjustment necessary to keep going when you start feeling defeated.

The Pursuit of Perfection implores you to let go of the idea that the perfect story or perfect manuscript exists. This idea alone has helped me no end in meeting my own writing goals; it's so much easier to sit down and write if you're shooting for a more manageable target than perfection.

The Write Attitude covers a number of different ways you can start making a difference in your writing by adjusting your expectations and, you guessed it, your attitude. Some of the material in *Couch to 50k* was inspired by this book but you should read in anyway because a) it never hurts to reinforce the thing you've learned and b) Kristine is a writer with forty-odd years experience in the publishing industry so, if you don't believe me when I say stuff you should definitely believe her.

30 Days in the Word Mines by Chuck Wendig

This is a NaNoWriMo specific set of advice and is a lovely little book in---how shall I put it?---Chuck's *inimitable* style. *30 Days in the Word Mines* will get you through each day of writing with advice, solidarity and encouragement. Sometimes it'll get you through by swearing at you a lot, but it'll get you through. Read it day by day during NaNoWriMo or put all of it in your eyes beforehand to prepare yourself for what is to come, it's up to you. But I definitely recommend reading this if you're ever gonna attempt 50,000 words in a 30 day stretch.

Writing into the Dark by Dean Wesley Smith

This is a book for the pantsers of the world. If you're not so much into the plotting and planning, instead preferring to go on a journey with your characters and see where the story takes you, this is the book for you. *Writing into the Dark* not only gives a great explanation for *why* you should write a novel without any prior planning—writing into the dark as Dean puts it—it also gives you a few strategies on how to approach that and how to get the most out of the experience.

Again, Dean is a very experienced writer; he's been making a living with his words since the 80s and has over a hundred novels under his belt, so he might know a thing or two about what he's talking about. If you're getting bogged down in what you *should* be doing when it comes to writing a novel, then this a good book for you to help you worry less about the conventions that are holding you back.

Take off Your Pants! Outline Your Books For Faster, Better Writing by Libbie Hawker

This one is for the plotters among us. Personally I'm not much of a plotter, but one of the reasons I like this book is that offers advice on different levels of planning out your novel. If you'd prefer a loose outline just so you know you're hitting all the major points in a story but there's still room for adventure and discovery as you write, this gives you a way of doing that. If you're the kind of person who likes to plan your stories down to the very last detail including what your main character is eating right before they go punch the big bad in the face then this book will help you too. Even if you're a pantser you can probably learn a thing or two from this book.

The Official NaNoWriMo Books

I haven't actually read either of these books myself, but I feel I would be remiss if I didn't mention them. *No Plot? No Problem* and *Ready, Set, Novel!* are available through the NaNoWriMo store and specifically geared towards people tackling the challenge. If you've bought

Couch to 50k to help prepare for NaNoWriMo then these books might also be useful.

Writing Communities

Community can be a really powerful thing when you're attempting a challenge like this, providing encouragement and motivation when you really need it.

But even though I strongly suggest dragging a friend along with you while you throw yourself head first into the word pit, that's not always possible. And sometimes even when it is, that's not the only thong you need.

That's when joining an online writing community can help.

I've been part of a few in my time, but here are some I recommend trying out.

The NaNoWriMo and Camp NaNoWriMo websites

This is without a doubt the best place to start when your looking for your fellow writers online. Using the NaNoWriMo websites will allow you to find writers who love on your time zone or local area, those who are at the same stage as you with their writing and people who love the same genres you do.

And the NaNoWriMo website has built in functionality to allow you to write alongside each other during November (or April and July for Camp

NaNoWriMo) so it's definitely worth checking out. This community is about more than just November, so get involved and see if you can't make a few new friends.

Inkwell Writers Mastermind Group

This is one of the friendliest groups I've been part of. Nicole Bianchi and the rest of the Inkwell Writers are super welcoming, no matter where you are in your journey. There are constant conversations in this group about goals and how you're getting on with your writing, plus Nicole herself regularly offers up useful advice. An overall great group.

Ninja Writers

Run by Shaunta Grimes, this is a great group for everyone from the beginning writer to the professional author. There are always people around to answer any questions you might have, and to help you unpick the knots in your novel. Ninja Writers also regularly band together to support each other outside of the group, so wherever you write, you can get your fellow Ninjas to cheer you on.

Not interested in doing NaNoWriMo?

This book is kind of geared towards people who want to take part in NaNoWriMo by it's very nature, but what if you're not one of them? What if you've tried the program and realised that writing over 1500 words a day for a month is just not something you want to try?

Well, fear not, you can still get something pretty cool out of the program.

If you want to complete NaNoWriMo after doing the standard Couch to 50k program, you need to do the final week to hit 50,000 words at 1700 words today. But if you decide that attempting NaNoWriMo isn't for you, or life gets in the way, like it so often does, and it gets pushed back to next year, you can still enjoy the accomplishment of having written 50,000 words. Instead of four more weeks at 1700 words a day, just do two more weeks at that amount to hit 53200 words in total.

You don't have to do them all at once, just write 1700 words a day for 14 days, whenever they fall.

On the fast track you need to write for 17 more days to cross the 50k mark and if you're doing the gentle program you just need to keep your pace for another four days to get there.

The point is, that while this book is designed explicitly for preparing to put 50,000 words onto paper during a single calendar month, but that's not the only possible application. Take what you've learned and make it your own, put it to work to help you meet *your* goals.

If I've done my job right, you can use this program to get to wherever you want to be with your writing. The only limit is your imagination and you're a writer; your imagination is limitless.

Remember that, and keep on writing.

SUMMARY

So you've reached the end of Couch to 50k. The book that is, not the program. Probably. At least not yet.

That means it's time to summarize everything and leave you with a final few pieces of advice and a pithy sound bite to round everything off. Let's get to it shall we?

Marathon Runners Train and Prepare, and So Should You

Over the last few chapters I hope I've stressed the importance of preparation when it comes to NaNoWriMo (or any other writing challenge for that matter). A runner wouldn't consider doing a marathon without training and preparation, and therefore neither should you attempt writing 50,000 words in a month without training and preparation.

NaNoWriMo really is the marathon of the writing world, and you should treat it accordingly.

Okay so sitting down and writing a few thousand words a day is a lot less physically demanding than running a marathon, but it's still work and it's still a shock to the system if you try to go from 0 to 1700 words a day all in one go. That's a recipe for RSI and burn out, which is never fun.

You need to build yourself up slowly, paying attention to your pacing and making sure you don't do too much at once. In the parable of the tortoise and the hare, you are the tortoise who successfully crosses the finish line because you've taken the time to prepare and made sure not to do too much at once. You've avoided burn out, unlike the hare, who tried to write 50,000 words as fast he physically could and ran out of energy to continue. The poor hare will probably never attempt any kind of writing challenge ever again.

Your Support Network Matters

I talked about how useful it can be to drag a friend or two along on your journey, to keep you company and so you can provide mutual encouragement for each other. If you can't convince any of your offline meatspace friends to take on the challenge of writing 50,000 words in a single month, it's worth seeking out online communities that can fulfil the same function. I've provided links to a few to help get you started.

If you do find a writing buddy to encourage, cajole or bribe you into getting your words done, be careful when it comes to comparing yourself to them. A little bit of competition when it comes to word count or writing streaks can be healthy, but be wary of negative comparisons.

It can be difficult to plod along doing your own thing if a writing buddy is writing way more words than you per day but remember; they are not you, and every writer is different. They might be writing at the optimum pace for them, or they might be on the road to burnout. You can't see inside their head so you don't know.

Know Thyself, and How You Write Best

What you can know is your own optimum conditions for writing. Experiment with where and when and how you do your writing. Play around with different software and writing sprints of different lengths. Find out what works for *you*.

This is all useful knowledge when NaNoWriMo comes around because you'll be in the best position to sit down every day and make those words happen. If you have a good idea of how many words per hour you can write under various conditions then you'll know roughly how much time you need to set aside to hit the daily word count for NaNoWriMo.

I also encourage experimenting with the total number of words per day that suit you as well. Sure, you might be able to sit down and blast out 5000 words at once, but how does that affect you afterwards? Does it mean you can't really write as much for a few days? Focus on finding the number of words you can comfortably hit in order to write every day and stick to that. You might need to push yourself above that for a challenge like NaNoWriMo, but if your looking to build a long term writing habit this kind of knowledge is crucial for goal setting.

Write it Down. It's Science If You Write It Down

No matter what your ideal writing conditions or number of words, I absolutely advocate keeping records of your writing. At a bare minimum, the total number of words written in a day. Having the concrete data to hand will not only help you with your pacing and goal setting and knowing your progress, it'll also act as a form of encouragement.

I was surprised when I started recording my word count by the way it quickly added up. Getting 500 words down in a day didn't feel like much, not when I saw people racking up thousands of words in a single day. But I kept going with my 500 words a day, doing more when I felt up to it and less when I felt off, and counted up what I'd done at the end of the month. It was more than I thought I'd written, let me tell you.

And keeping a record of my writing progress has really helped me meet my goals. Just like writing 50,000 words in a month is a lot less scary if you break it down, writing a novel fells less intimidating when you shift your focus from "oh god I have to write 90,000 words holy shit" to just getting your words down for the day.

Focus on the daily habit, and the big stuff will take care of itself.

Keep Yourself Honest. Are You Actually Writing?

Also, be honest with yourself about what counts as writing. Don't fool yourself into thinking you've made progress when you haven't.

The only thing that counts as writing, the only thing that should be going in your records as writing is adding new words to a project in such a way that the overall word count increases. That's it. It's that simple, and that hard. Anything else is just kidding yourself.

Editing is not writing.

Planning is not writing.

Checking social media definitely isn't writing.

Only keep records of what actually counts as writing. Other activities may be useful and necessary for writing, but they are not writing. Only by being completely honest with yourself will you make progress and hit your goals. It's the only way you'll be able to step up and write 50,000 words in a month.

Do The Program, See the Results

I've given you a program to help prepare you for that challenge. Well, three of them actually, so you can choose-your-own-adventure and pick the pace that is right for you. The actual Couch to 50k program is where everything I've said in this book gets put into action.

Use the program to train for NaNoWriMo. Use it to get back to writing after time off because Life got in the way. Use it to build up the speed and stamina you need to write the words necessary to start a writing career.

Yes, Couch to 50k is absolutely geared towards people looking to do NaNoWriMo, but both the program and the mindset it promotes can be used to reach almost any writing goal. And I promise you, if you can write 50,000 words in a month without experiencing burn out, you have the skills and habits to hit any writing goal you care to set yourself.

The world is your bivalve mollusc. I believe in you. You can write whatever you want.

The Tools For Success

I've haven't just provided you with the Couch to 50k program and left you to get on with it though. I've also given you the tools you need to really succeed at writing 50,000 words in a month. Spreadsheets and word tracker to help you keep a record of your word counts in the way that's most useful to you. Book recommendation for after you finish this one, books that I've found useful in my own writing. Links to writing communities that will provide advice and encouragement and where there are other people going through exactly the same things you are.

I hope though, that the most useful tool I've given you is the knowledge that you can do it. You really can write 50,000 words in a single month. If you take it seriously, properly prepare and train, and pace yourself, there's no reason to believe you won't succeed.

Writing 50,000 words in a single month is a heck of an ask. It's not to be sniffed at. But what you have here in this book are the tools you need to get you there. And you have the tools to build up your confidence in your writing and make positive habits that will get you through NaNoWriMo and beyond.

I've given you the tools you need to find small victories that will spur you on to larger ones, and the data to prove to yourself you can do it. Keep putting one foot in front of the other, one word after another, and you'll get there.

Focus on Quantity, Quality Will Come

One thing I haven't spoken about in this book is the *quality* of the words that you write. The focus of Couch to 50k is simply getting the quantity down. The quality doesn't matter.

Why?

Because the quality will come with practice. And that's exactly what this is about, building a habit and a practice. Every word you write is practice and the more words you write, the better they will be. The more comfortable you will be with them and the more you will settle into your own style.

The focus of Couch to 50k is the quantity of words you're producing because quality is a function of quantity. Focus on getting the words out and the quality will come.

Don't believe me? Try writing every day for a month and compare what you wrote on the first day with what you write on the last day. I guarantee you will be happier with what you wrote after a month of practice than what you wrote before.

You *Will* Succeed

I want to finish this book by saying that what you've set out to do isn't easy. Writing 50,000 words in a month is a hell of a thing to aim for, especially if you have a family and a day job to work around. When you get there, and I do believe it's a matter of *when*, you should be proud of yourself. You have every right to be.

Runners who complete a marathon get a medal. Sadly there are no medals for NaNoWriMo, but you certainly deserve one. When you cross that finish line you will have done what so many people set out to do but don't. You said you'd write 50,000 words in a month and you did. That's enough words to write a novel, that elusive thing probably millions of us say we want to do but very few actually do.

You have what it takes to write a novel. You have the tools you need to get you there. I look forward to reading the finished product.

About The Author

Rachel Tonks Hill, always wanted to be either a doctor or writer when she grew up. She wrote her first novel as procrastination from her doctoral thesis. Her latest novel, Novis, was released in 2018. While she has definitely fulfilled her dream, she hopes this doesn't mean she has to grow up. Rachel lives in Nottingham with her partner and insufficient dogs.

racheltonkshill.com

facebook.com/racheltonkshill

twitter: @captainraz

OTHER BOOKS BY THE AUTHOR

On the Rise (Penumbra Book 1)

The Whisper of the Leaves (Daughter of Duri Book 1)

Novis

Beyond the Edge of Reason

Objective Reasoning

The Emerald Mist

12 Stories in 12 Hours

In Short: A Flash Fiction Collection

On A Dark Wave, Floundering

Printed in Great Britain
by Amazon